UNDERSTANDING ELECTRICITY

© Aladdin Books Ltd 2010

Published in the United States in 2010 by
Stargazer Books, distributed by
Black Rabbit Books
P.O. Box 3263
Mankato, MN 56002

Illustrator: Tony Kenyon

Printed in the United States

Library of Congress Cataloging-in-Publication Data

Gibson, Gary, 1957-
  Understanding electricity / Gary Gibson.
     p. cm. -- (Fun science projects)
  Includes index.
  ISBN 978-1-59604-194-3
 1. Electricity--Juvenile literature. 2. Electricity--Experiments--Juvenile
literature. I. Title.
  QC527.2.G522 2009
  537--dc22

                                                        2008016401

Fun Science Projects
UNDERSTANDING ELECTRICITY

GARY GIBSON

Stargazer Books
Mankato, Minnesota

CONTENTS

INTRODUCTION

Can you imagine a world without electricity? There would be no electric lights and no battery-powered objects like radios and calculators. Electricity is everywhere. We cook our food in electric ovens, and we keep food cold in refrigerators powered by electricity. The battery in a car starts the engine. Most home entertainment—from television and DVDs, to music and computers—is powered by electricity. This book contains many hands-on projects that help explain how electricity works.

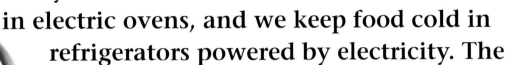

When this symbol appears, adult supervision is required.

WHAT IS ELECTRICITY?

All things are made up of tiny particles called atoms. Atoms are made from even smaller particles, some of which are electrically charged. This charge may be negative or positive. Electricity is a flow of the negatively-charged particles. You can see a flow of charge in the form of a spark.

MAKE A FISHING GAME

1 Find a metal tray or a cookie tin lid. Place a lump of clay, large enough to use as a handle, in the middle of the tray.

2 Place the tray on a large plastic bag. Grip the clay firmly with one hand, press down, and rotate the tray vigorously for two minutes on the plastic.

3 Be very careful not to touch the tray with your hands. Lift the tray off the plastic with the clay grip.

4 Pick up a metal fork with your free hand. Touch the edge of the tray with it. Hear the sparks crackle!

WHY IT WORKS

As the tray is rubbed on the plastic, it becomes negatively-charged. The fork is positively-charged, and when it is brought close to the tray it attracts the negative charges. They jump through the air to the fork as a spark.

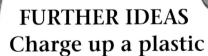

FURTHER IDEAS
Charge up a plastic comb by rubbing it vigorously on a clean, dry cloth. Adjust a faucet to give a thin stream of running water. Bring the comb close to the stream. The comb pulls at the water! Make the water dance by jiggling the comb.

STATIC ELECTRICITY

The ancient Greeks noticed that when amber (fossilized tree resin) is rubbed, it attracts light objects, such as feathers. This is because the amber has become electrically charged. The word *electricity* comes from the Greek word *elektron*, meaning amber. Scientists use an electroscope to check if an object is electrically charged.

MAKE AN ELECTROSCOPE

1 Cut a circle of cardboard big enough to fit over the top of a clean glass jar. Cut two ½-inch (1-cm) -long parallel slots in the middle of the cardboard.

2 Cut out two strips of aluminum foil. They should be about ½ in (1 cm) wide and 2 in (5 cm) long.

3 Insert one strip through each slot so the strips overlap at the top. Tape the cardboard to the top of the jar so the strips hang downward.

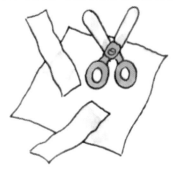

4 Charge up a plastic comb by rubbing it vigorously for a couple of minutes with a clean, dry cloth.

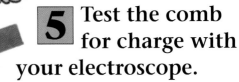

5 Test the comb for charge with your electroscope. Touch the top of the aluminum strips with the comb. Watch what happens to the two strips.

WHY IT WORKS

Electricity cannot move through plastic or amber. But they can hold a static (not moving) electric charge. When the comb touches the strips, the electric charge is released because electricity can move through metal. Both strips receive the same kind of charge, and because like charges push each other away, the strips move apart.

FURTHER IDEAS

Inflate two balloons. Tie a piece of nylon thread to the end of each balloon. Rub each balloon on a woolen sweater. Hang both balloons together from their threads. Watch how they push each other away.

BATTERY POWER

Static electricity is not very useful for powering machines, so we use *current* electricity. An electric current is a controlled flow of electric charge. Batteries produce electric currents from chemicals.

Alessandro Volta made the first battery in 1800. The volt, a unit of electric measurement, is named after him.

MAKE A BATTERY

1 Find 12 copper coins and zinc washers of similar size. They will need to be stacked. Cut out 12 same-sized circles of blotting paper.

2 Pour vinegar into a glass with a tablespoonful of salt. Soak each piece of blotting paper in the mixture. Stack a coin, then a washer, then a piece of blotting paper. Finish with a washer.

3 Take six and a half feet (2m) of thin plastic-coated copper wire. Coil it tightly around an iron nail as many times as you can.

4 Attach one end of the copper wire to the bottom coin and the other to the top washer.

5 Test your battery by bringing the nail close to a small compass. The nail should make the compass needle spin.

WHY IT WORKS

The salt and vinegar start a chemical reaction. Negatively-charged particles flow through the coins to the washers, around the wire coil, and back to the battery. The electric current creates a magnetic field that affects a compass needle (see pages 26–27).

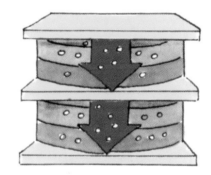

FURTHER IDEAS
Find a juicy lemon. Push one copper and one zinc nail into it. Touch both nails with your tongue. You will feel a tingle from the flow of current in the lemon "battery."

SIMPLE CIRCUITS

The path an electric current takes is called a circuit. Electric current flows from the power supply, to the lightbulb, and back to the power supply. As long as there are no gaps in the circuit, the electric current will flow.

MAKE A CIRCUIT

1 Ask an adult to open up a coat hanger. Bend it into a wavy shape. Push the ends of the wire into a cardboard base. Hold each end in place with clay.

2 Make a loop out of thin wire. Connect it to a long piece of insulated wire. Thread this through a plastic straw to form a handle. Slip the loop onto the wavy wire.

3 Attach a 6-volt lightbulb and a 6-volt battery to the base. Wire the battery and bulb to the wavy wire as shown (right).

4 Connect the other end of the bulb to the loop. The wire needs to be long enough to reach both ends of the wavy wire.

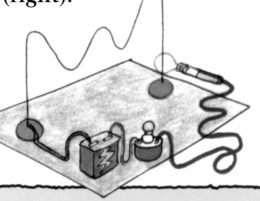

5 Check that the bulb lights when you touch the loop to the wavy wire. Now try and move the loop along the path of the wavy wire without letting the two touch!

WHY IT WORKS

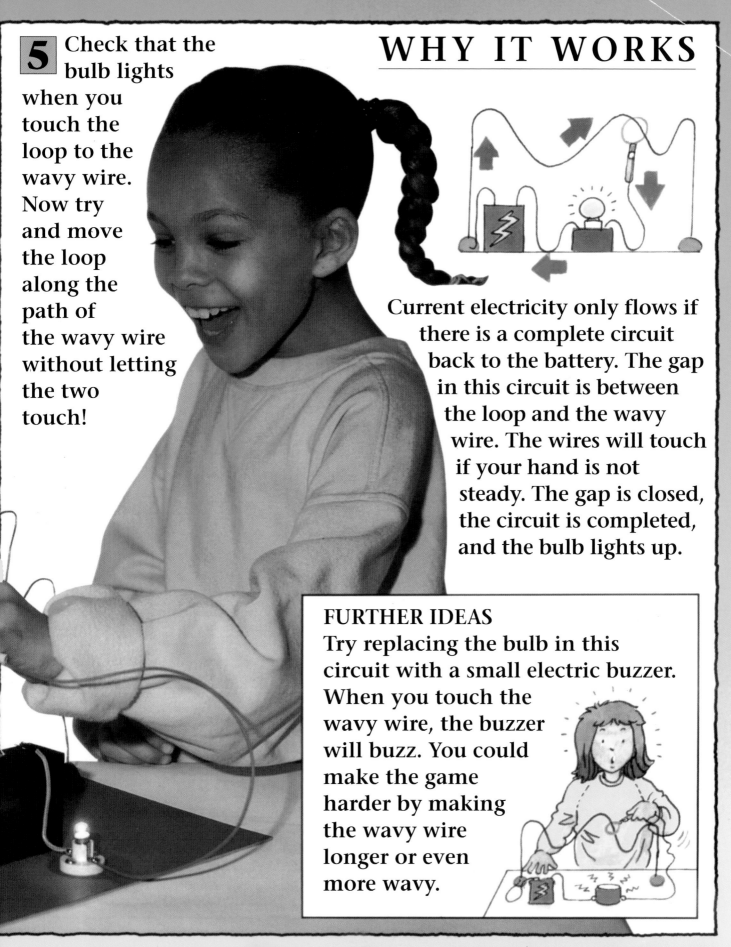

Current electricity only flows if there is a complete circuit back to the battery. The gap in this circuit is between the loop and the wavy wire. The wires will touch if your hand is not steady. The gap is closed, the circuit is completed, and the bulb lights up.

FURTHER IDEAS
Try replacing the bulb in this circuit with a small electric buzzer. When you touch the wavy wire, the buzzer will buzz. You could make the game harder by making the wavy wire longer or even more wavy.

CONDUCTORS AND INSULATORS

Some materials allow electricity to flow through them easily. These materials are called electrical conductors. Most metals are good conductors. Other materials, like plastic, do not easily let electricity flow through them. These materials, called insulators, are used to prevent electricity from reaching places where it would be dangerous.

TEST FOR ELECTRICAL CONDUCTORS

1 Find a thick cardboard base. Cut out two squares of aluminum foil. Glue them onto the base. Leave a small gap between them (see right).

2 Attach a piece of thin plastic-coated copper wire to one square. Glue it to the board as shown. Repeat for the other side.

3 Connect one of the wires to a 6-volt lightbulb (right). Glue the bulb to the base.

4 Connect the other wire to a 6-volt battery. Now connect the battery and the bulb to a small plastic-coated copper wire.

5 Test a range of objects, such as keys, pencils, or erasers, by placing them across the two squares.

WHY IT WORKS

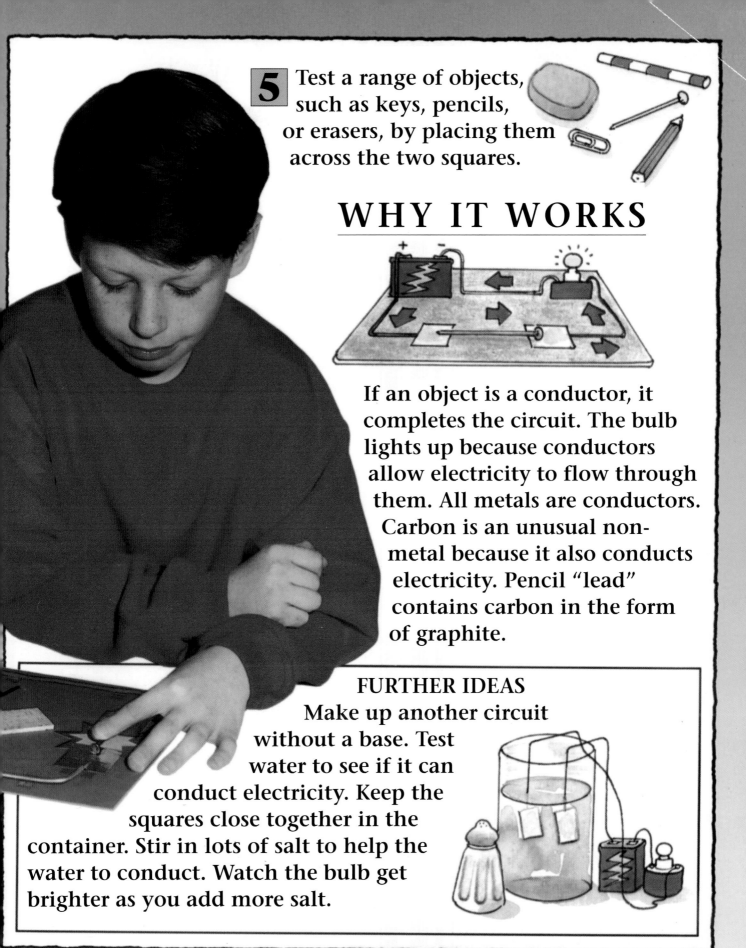

If an object is a conductor, it completes the circuit. The bulb lights up because conductors allow electricity to flow through them. All metals are conductors. Carbon is an unusual non-metal because it also conducts electricity. Pencil "lead" contains carbon in the form of graphite.

FURTHER IDEAS

Make up another circuit without a base. Test water to see if it can conduct electricity. Keep the squares close together in the container. Stir in lots of salt to help the water to conduct. Watch the bulb get brighter as you add more salt.

RESISTANCE

Good conductors of electricity allow electricity to flow easily. A thick wire can conduct more electricity than a thin wire, just like a wide road can carry more cars than a narrow road. The thin wire resists the flow of electricity or has a higher resistance.

MAKE A DIMMER SWITCH

1 Attach a 6-volt battery and 6-volt bulb to a thick cardboard base. Use two long wires and one short one to make a circuit as shown (right).

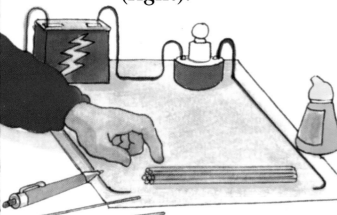

2 Remove the graphite from a mechanical pencil. Tape or glue together half a dozen graphite rods. Attach the wire from the battery to the bundle.

3 Attach a square of aluminum foil to the wire from the bulb. Check that the circuit is complete and the bulb lights when you touch the square to the graphite.

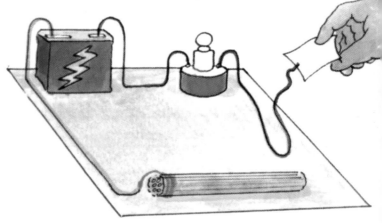

WHY IT WORKS

Graphite is made of carbon, which is a conductor. As you slide the square along the graphite toward the battery, the electricity travels less distance. This means less resistance, so the bulb gets brighter.

4 Slide the aluminum square along the graphite from one end to the other. Watch the lightbulb.

FURTHER IDEAS
Make a circuit (right). Attach two non-silver spoons. Stir a spoonful of salt into a bowl of water. Put the spoons in the water. Watch the bulb as you move the spoons apart.

OPEN CIRCUITS

Every time you turn on a light you are completing a circuit. As soon as a switch is closed (turned on), the circuit is completed and the electricity operates the bulb or electrical appliance. In 1837, Samuel Morse had the idea of completing and breaking an electrical circuit to send messages.

SEND A MESSAGE

1 Make a circuit using a 6-volt battery and 6-volt bulb attached to a thick cardboard base. Leave a gap between the two wires (see left).

2 Make a switch out of a steel paper clip. Attach it to the end of the wire running from the battery. Tape a square of aluminum foil over the top (see right). Tape another aluminum square over the end of the other wire. Make sure the paper clip reaches this square.

3 Press the paper clip down to touch the square and switch on the bulb. Practice long and short flashes to send a Morse code message.

WHY IT WORKS

Electricity cannot flow when a circuit is open. Closing the switch completes the circuit. The bulb lights immediately because electricity can travel so quickly.

FURTHER IDEAS Make a burglar alarm using your circuit board as a base. Tape some pencils or straws along the side edges. Place a second board on top of the pencils leaving the bulb and battery clear. Cover the boards with a mat. When the "intruder" steps on the mat, the switch will be pressed and the burglar alarm will light up.

TURNED ON

Being able to turn a light on or off from two different places can be very useful. If a light can be turned on or off from both the top and the bottom of a staircase then not only is it safer at night but energy is also saved. This kind of switch is called a two-way switch.

MAKE A TWO-WAY SWITCH

1 Fold a piece of cardboard into a wedge shape (shown right). Draw a line down the center. Stick down two pieces of cardboard on each side of the line and draw a staircase.

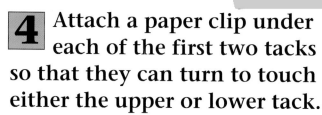

2 Make a circuit using a 6-volt battery and light-bulb. Push a tack through each piece of cardboard. Attach the wires to them.

3 Push four more tacks into the cardboard (shown below). Connect the upper two with a short piece of wire and repeat for the lower two.

4 Attach a paper clip under each of the first two tacks so that they can turn to touch either the upper or lower tack.

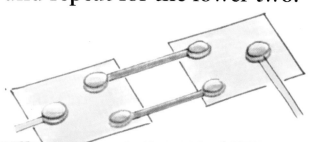

WHY IT WORKS

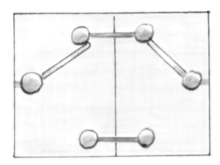 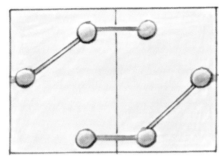 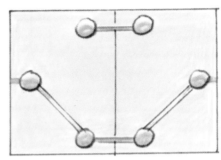

The two-way switch allows two alternative paths for an electric current. Electricity can flow only when both paper clips are touching the same wire. Removing one of the paper clips from the wire breaks the circuit.

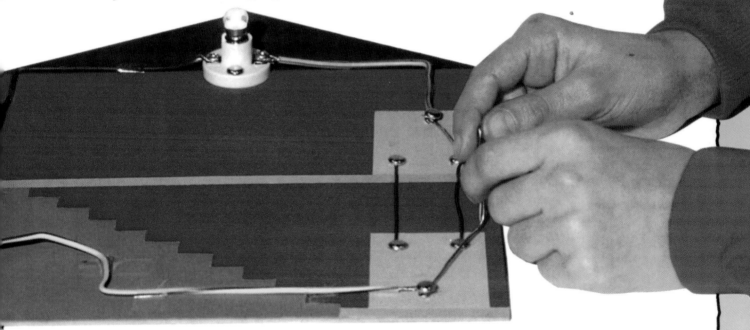

5 Turn the switches on and off. Both paper clips must touch one of the two tacks to make a circuit.

FURTHER IDEAS Make a three-way switch quiz game (see right). When the paper clips point to the same letter, the bulb lights up. When your friend chooses the correct answer (a, b, or c), the bulb lights up.

BIGGER CIRCUITS

All the circuits you have built so far have been small and simple, requiring only one piece of wire. Electric circuits in your home consist of many more wires. Finding which wire is connected to which source can be like finding your way through a maze.

MAKE A MAZE

1 Find a large piece of thick cardboard. Cut out ½-in (1-cm) -wide strips of aluminum foil about the same length as the cardboard.

2 Flatten the aluminum strips, glue them to the cardboard, then make a criss-cross pattern with the strips.

3 Attach a 6-in (15-cm) -long wire to one side of a 6-volt bulb. Now attach a 3.5-ft (1-m) -long wire to a dowel pointer, leaving the copper exposed at the end.

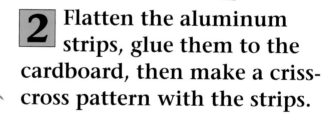

4 Make a circuit (left). Wire the battery to the aluminum at one corner of the board. Test the circuit by touching the pointer to the foil.

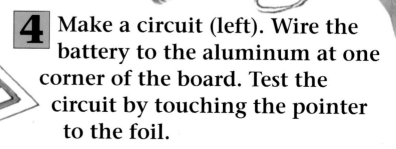

5 Cover parts of the aluminum with insulating tape. Copy the pattern shown at the bottom of the page. The gray shaded areas show where the tape should go.

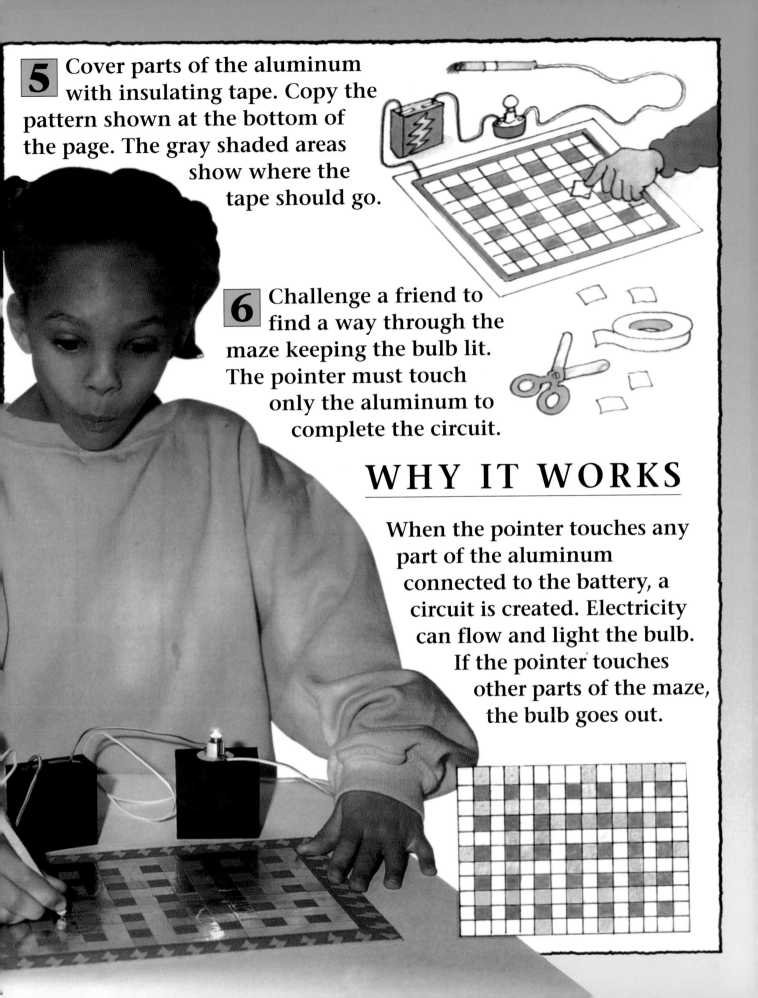

6 Challenge a friend to find a way through the maze keeping the bulb lit. The pointer must touch only the aluminum to complete the circuit.

WHY IT WORKS

When the pointer touches any part of the aluminum connected to the battery, a circuit is created. Electricity can flow and light the bulb. If the pointer touches other parts of the maze, the bulb goes out.

HOUSE LIGHTS

A simple way to arrange more than one lightbulb is in a series, so the electricity flows through one bulb to the next. But if a bulb fails, the circuit is broken, and all the lights go out. In a parallel circuit, each bulb has its own connection to the battery, so if one bulb fails the others are unaffected. House lights work this way.

MAKE A RING CIRCUIT

1 Ask an adult to bend two pieces of wire into two rings, one larger than the other. Use some cardboard as a base for your circuit.

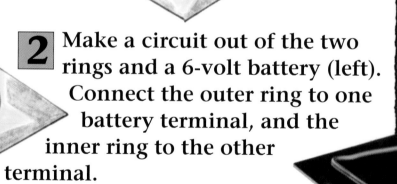

2 Make a circuit out of the two rings and a 6-volt battery (left). Connect the outer ring to one battery terminal, and the inner ring to the other terminal.

3 Connect two pieces of thin plastic-coated copper wire to the ends of a 6-volt bulb. Check that there is plenty of bare wire showing at the free ends.

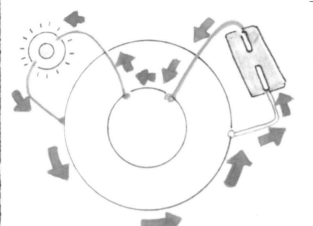

Wherever the battery and bulb are placed on the rings, there is always a complete circuit. This type of parallel circuit is called a ring circuit.

4 Attach one of the wires running from the lightbulb to the outer ring, and one to the inner ring. It forms a circuit and the bulb lights up.

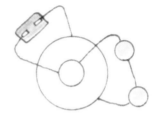

FURTHER IDEAS
Try adding another bulb to your ring circuit. Does one affect the other? Can you find a place on the rings where the circuit does not work?

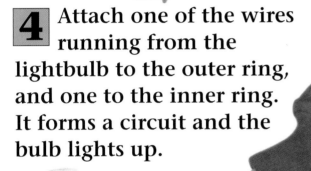

MOVEMENT FROM ELECTRICITY

Electric motors do all sorts of useful work in the home. They are found in household items such as washing machines, electric heaters, and food processors. The movement produced is usually a spinning motion. The electric motor uses electricity and magnetism to produce movements.

MAKE A SIMPLE MOTOR

1 Wrap four 3.5 ft (1 m) pieces of wire together to form a loop (see right). Secure the wires with insulation tape.

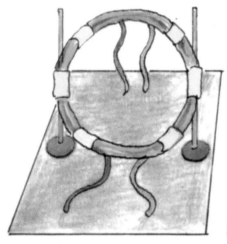 

2 On a cardboard base, attach two dowels in an upright position with clay. Next, tape the wire to the dowels (as shown above).

3 Attach the two top wires to a 6-volt battery. Attach the bottom wires to two aluminum squares at the base. Make a switch out of a paper clip.

4 Leave the switch open. Hold a small pocket compass level in the middle of the wire loop. Note the direction the compass points to.

5 Now turn off the switch and watch the effect on the compass. It should spin around until you turn the switch on again.

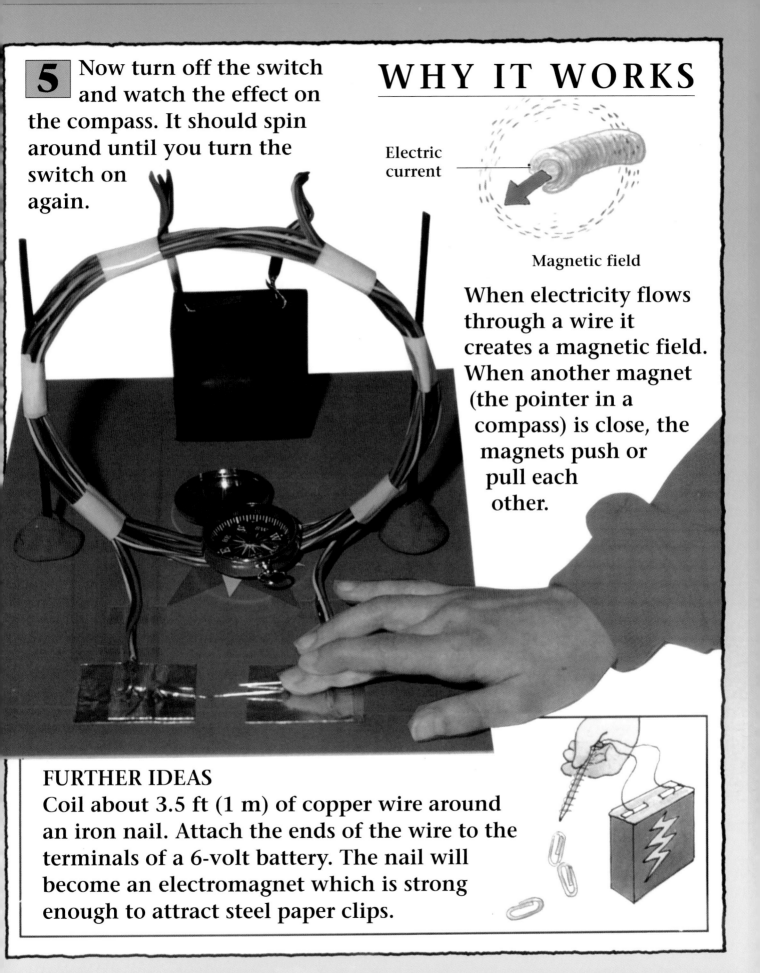

Electric current

Magnetic field

When electricity flows through a wire it creates a magnetic field. When another magnet (the pointer in a compass) is close, the magnets push or pull each other.

FURTHER IDEAS
Coil about 3.5 ft (1 m) of copper wire around an iron nail. Attach the ends of the wire to the terminals of a 6-volt battery. The nail will become an electromagnet which is strong enough to attract steel paper clips.

ELECTROPLATING

An electric current can be used to split chemicals into the elements that they are made of. If an electric current is passed through a liquid called an electrolyte, charged particles will move through it. This is called electrolysis. Cutlery and jewelry are silverplated using electrolysis.

COPPERPLATE A SILVER COIN

1 Fill a clean glass jar with water. This will act as your electrolyte.

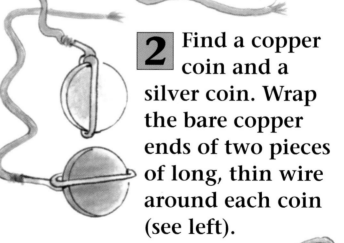

2 Find a copper coin and a silver coin. Wrap the bare copper ends of two pieces of long, thin wire around each coin (see left).

3 Put the coins into the water. Wrap the two wires around a pencil balanced over the top of the jar (see below).

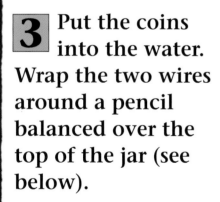

4 Connect the copper coin to the positive (+) terminal of a 6-volt battery, and the silver coin to the negative (-) terminal.

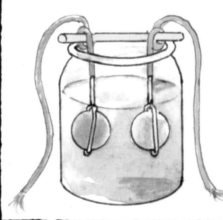

5 Make sure the coins are close but not touching. Leave the circuit set up for five minutes. Take out the two coins and observe.

WHY IT WORKS

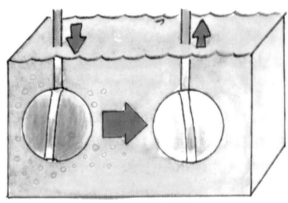

Electric current enters the water through the positive terminal attached to the copper coin. It carries some of the copper with it. The current carries the copper through the water to the silver coin. The copper is left as a thin layer over the silver coin. The copper can easily be scraped off afterward. Dispose of the water carefully because it is poisonous.

FURTHER IDEAS
Try using vinegar with lots of salt stirred into it as the electrolyte instead of water. Using a more powerful battery produces faster and thicker plating.

FANTASTIC ELECTRICITY FACTS

The first man to prove that lightning is electricity was Benjamin Franklin. In 1752, he flew a kite during a thunderstorm. Lightning struck the kite and traveled down its wet string to a key fastened to the end, where the lightning caused sparks.

In about 1820, Michael Faraday let a wire coil carrying an electric current dangle near a magnet. When the electricity flowed through the wire, it moved, circling around and around the magnet. This was the principle of the electric motor.

In about 1876, Alexander Graham Bell made a machine that changed sounds into electrical signals. This was the first telephone.

The electric lightbulb was invented in 1879 by Thomas Edison. Three years later, U.S. factories made 100,000 bulbs. By 1900, production reached over 35 million.

Italian professor Alessandro Volta made the first battery to give a steady flow of electric current in 1800. The most durable battery was made in 1840, by Watlin and Hill, instrument makers in England. The battery has been working at a lab in England ever since.

In 1888, the German scientist Heinrich Hertz built an electrical machine that could detect waves given off by an electric current. This machine made a sound when the waves were detected. This was the first radio transmission.

The most powerful electric current ever was generated by scientists at the Los Alamos laboratory in New Mexico. For a few milliseconds they produced twice as much current as the total amount of electricity being produced elsewhere on Earth.

In the early 1970s, astronauts drove around on the moon in the Lunar Rover. It had electric motors and a top speed of 8 miles per hour (13 kph).

GLOSSARY

Atom
The smallest complete particle that everything is made up of. Atoms are made up of smaller particles called electrons, protons, and neutrons.

Charge
Electric charge can be either positive or negative. Inside atoms, electrons carry a negative charge and protons carry a positive charge.

Circuit
A complete path around which an electric current can flow.

Conductor
Any material that allows electricity to pass through it.

Current
A flow of negative charge (electrons) around a circuit.

Electric motor
A machine that turns electricity into movement by using a magnet.

Electrolyte
A liquid in which a chemical reaction takes place when an electric current flows through it.

Electron
A negatively-charged particle even smaller than an atom.

Electroscope
A device used by scientists to measure how much static electricity an object contains.

Insulator
Any material that does not let electricity pass through it.

Magnetic field
The area around a magnet where the magnetic effects are felt.

Resistance
The ability that a material has to stop or resist the flow of electric current through it.

Terminal
The part of a battery to which wires can be attached.

INDEX